GEORGE WASHINGTON CARVER

The Genius Behind the Peanut

by Camilla J. Wilson

AN
APPLE
PAPERBACK

SCHOLASTIC INC.
New York   Toronto   London   Auckland   Sydney
Mexico City   New Delhi   Hong Kong   Buenos Aires

ISBN 0-439-28722-7

Text copyright © 2003 by Camilla J. Wilson.
All rights reserved. Published by Scholastic Inc.

SCHOLASTIC, APPLE PAPERBACKS, and associated
logos are trademarks and/or registered trademarks of
Scholastic Inc.

12 11 10 9 8 7 6 5 4 3   4 5 6 7 8/0

Printed in the U.S.A.   40

First printing, February 2003

Dedicated to all the members of my family who especially love the soil; in particular, this love of dirt enticed my father, Kenneth Wilson, and his parents, Dewey and Susie Wilson, as well as my grandfather on my mother's side, Luther B. Lee.

Table of Contents

Acknowledgments

I have been blessed with the support and assistance of numerous people on this project. In particular, I would like to thank Dr. Linda Ferreira, editorial director at Scholastic, for discussing the possibility of a book on George Washington Carver. I would like to thank Gina Shaw, my editor, for all her assistance and patience, as well as Rachel Lisberg, the editorial assistant who contributed so much to this effort.

The staff of the George Washington Carver Museum at Tuskegee University and the library there provided me with ongoing assistance. The George Washington Carver National Monument in Diamond, Missouri, likewise provided much material to me. Park Ranger Diane Eilenstein, in particular, contributed special information about Carver and about resources available in the 210-acre park administered by the National Park Service.

Dr. Marian Huttenstine encouraged my project, and Donna Blair dispensed critical assistance on numerous occasions.

Rod Miller provided excellent research assistance. Judith Adams, Kate Permenter, Eric Johnson, and Merry George provided a much-needed cheering squad. My daughter, Leigh Wilson-Mattson, provided special critical assistance.

I thank you all.

Camilla J. Wilson
Moorhead, Minnesota
August 29, 2002

Introduction

There was a lot that the small, sickly boy didn't have. He didn't have parents. He hardly ever saw money, and only on the rarest occasions did he have a penny to spend. Store-bought toys were out of the question. He lived on a farm with a family who stayed mostly to themselves.

Besides, as a barely freed slave, he was not expected to play or buy or learn. The few schools in the area would not admit him anyway: He was just "Carver's George," a youngster on the Moses Carver homestead.

"Carver's George" was African-American. In southern Missouri in the 1870s, that meant that the only expectation for him was that he would work. He would do whatever his master told him to do, from dawn to dark or later. He would eat whatever food he was given, sleep where he was told, and wear whatever clothing was handed down. And he was to be cheerful.

The child, who would later name himself George Washington Carver, *was* cheerful. He was also incredibly curious and he filled his pockets with the treasures he found everywhere he went.

To Carver's amazement, others did not recognize treasure when they saw it. No matter. That just meant more "beauties" for his secret garden, the hidden-away place he fashioned in the woods. His garden was a safe spot where he could take special plants and critters and his precious rock collection.

He built a play yard for his collection of frogs, which had been banished from the house. He hummed and talked to his plants, and they bloomed and grew for him. He even managed to get his favorite plants through the harsh winters by building a little cellar for them.

The plants and the animals paid Carver back in their own way. He learned how they reacted to different soils, how much water and sunlight they liked. He felt carefully along their leaves, looking for pests and signs of sickness. In later years, he would say they told him their secrets.

Carver had an endless list of questions: What makes it rain, and why do sunflowers grow so tall? Where does the sun go at night, and why do bees like honey so much?

It was George Washington Carver's yearning for knowledge that would allow him to grow up to fashion a life of great accomplishment and worldwide fame.

Like Rumplestiltskin, the fairy-tale character who spun straw into gold, George Washington Carver took dirt, rocks, and plants and created hundreds of new products, more than three hundred from peanuts alone. Every day, millions of people may use foods and crayons, dyes and plastics that Carver had a part in pioneering. Countless children in the United States have packed a school lunch using one of Carver's favorite creations: peanut butter.

Many of Carver's ideas, particularly on farming, were so advanced they have just begun to catch on in recent decades. Yet it all began with the birth of an infant to a slave mother on a farm on the Missouri frontier, late in the American Civil War.

1

Kidnapped . . . and Left for Dead

The day the kidnappers came, George Washington Carver's mother just wouldn't let go.

When the horses clattered up into the yard of the "little one-roomed log shanty," as Carver later described the place he was born, Mary Carver was terror-stricken. This was the third time bushwhackers had descended on the farm. Each time was more horrific than the time before. She snatched up her infant, George, and tried to run. Then they grabbed her.

Rough men shouted and cursed. Horses reared and whinnied. Across the yard, Moses Carver managed to grab Mary's older son, Jim, and flee to the woods. Tears, shrieks, moans. They threw Mary, still clutching her baby, atop a horse and fled.

None of the lives of the Carver family would ever be the same again.

Being a slave had been only one of life's problems for the thin, sickly baby who now bounced along on a horse, kidnapped by ruffians, feeling his mother's terror even as she clutched him close.

He had been born at a bad time in history, in an especially dangerous area, and into a slaveholding white family. Under the circumstances, there was little likelihood that the infant would survive.

The American Civil War (1861–1865) raged in Carver's neighborhood even as it pulled the nation apart. His mother had been purchased from a neighboring farm by a middle-aged German couple when she was only thirteen years old.

No one bothered to keep careful records of slave births or ages, so the exact date of Carver's birth is unknown. Carver himself repeatedly said he was born in 1864, shortly before the end of the Civil War, but some census records indicate he may have been born earlier.

Moses Carver was a German settler who

had moved to the southwestern corner of Missouri from Ohio and Illinois. He bought Mary, even though he considered himself to be antislavery and pro-Union. Moses and Susan Carver had no children, and the nephews they'd raised had moved out and left them with no help. So Moses Carver hired a man to help him and then bought Mary in 1855 to help Susan Carver.

During the next nine years, Mary had two, perhaps four children. Her oldest, Jim, was born in 1859, according to the tombstone Moses Carver later erected for the young man, who died in a smallpox outbreak in 1883 in Seneca, Missouri. George Washington Carver also referred, at times, to two sisters who died young.

The farm was in a community that was known as Diamond Grove, named for a diamond-shaped group of trees where a settlement grew, not far from the Carver farm. The village had few structures: a blacksmith shop and post office, a general store, and a church that also served as a school.

Diamond Grove and the surrounding counties were particularly unsafe. Missouri was a border state, located between the warring pro-slavery Confederate states to the south and the antislavery Union states to the north. Missouri was a slaveholding state, but large groups of European immigrants had moved into the state and helped to sway the vote to stay in the Union.

This infuriated Missouri residents who backed the Confederacy. Roving bands of soldiers, both Confederate and Union, roamed southern Missouri and often clashed. Even families were divided over the war, with brother fighting brother.

Sometimes troops took over towns, looted farms, killed or stole the livestock, and then moved on. Before long, a unit from the other side might show up and repeat the same actions. Farmers hid their cows and horses in the woods when they could, buried food and money, and tried their best to survive.

Local settlers had plenty of differences even before the Civil War began. Several families often moved into an area and staked out adjoining farms. They wrote letters back to where they came from — often making the new land sound better than it was — and before long other family members or old neighbors might arrive.

People from Ohio and Illinois pioneered the area north of Diamond Grove. German,

Swiss, and Polish immigrants lived in the central area of the region, while southerners from Tennessee lived to the south.

In addition, three widely varying states were within twenty-five miles of the Carver farm, and the problems common to each state frequently spilled over into the Carvers' little corner of Missouri.

First, there was Arkansas, a slaveholding state that had left the Union and joined the Confederacy. Second, there was Kansas, a free state during the war but which had been settled by groups of violent people who often battled one another over the slavery issue and then fled over state lines. Finally, there was Oklahoma, the Indian Territory, where U.S. law did not apply, and bands of outlaws roamed free. They probably caused the most trouble of all.

With men often away in either the Confederate or the Union armies, robbers preyed on the farms where women, older family members, and children were trying to survive. They kidnapped women and children. They stole horses and looted homesteads. If they found slaves, they rounded them up and rode off with them. They could sell slaves for a high price in Arkansas.

Moses Carver was a particular target in the community. Many of his own neighbors were annoyed with him. He kept to himself. He did not like organized religion. He owned slaves (Mary and her children), yet he opposed slavery and supported the Union in the Civil War. Thus, he offended Unionists by owning slaves, and he offended slaveholding supporters by being a Union man.

Moreover, Moses Carver was a prosperous farmer, and he was known to have money. Bandits came calling at the Carver farm at least three times. The second time, they almost killed him.

In 1863, during the fall or winter, bushwhackers showed up at the Carver farm and demanded all his money. When Moses Carver refused to cooperate, the ruffians strung him up to a tree. Then they placed hot coals on his feet. Eventually, the men searched the farm and left. But the Carver family lived in terror: They were sure the scoundrels would be back.

And in 1864, not long after Mary delivered her new baby, George, the bushwhackers came again. This time they were after slaves, whom they could take to the nearby slaveholding state of Arkansas or sell to soldiers of either the Union or Confederate armies, both of which also had units in the area.

Moses Carver said he heard horses and then screams. He managed to grab Mary's older son, Jim, and they hid.

Mary and George were not so lucky, as they were thrown on a horse and taken away.

"(I was) stolen . . . a wee babe in her arms," George Washington Carver would say much later in life.

Moses Carver did everything he could to get Mary and baby George back. He hired a local man with contacts in outlaw gangs to go after the two. Carver offered the pursuer land and a racehorse if he succeeded.

Eventually, the man came back with the baby in a saddlebag. The child was nearly dead, wracked with whooping cough. The thieves had discarded the baby, leaving it with some women along the way. They had taken Mary south toward Arkansas, he informed Moses Carver. Later, the Carvers heard rumors that the bandits might have sold Mary to soldiers going north. Regardless, she was gone forever from her children.

Heartsick, Moses Carver paid the rescuer

with a fine racehorse and handed the filthy bundle of rags over to his wife, Susan.

Susan Carver took the infant into the Carver cabin, where she'd taken his brother, Jim, after the kidnapping. She warmed some milk for the baby and slowly nursed the child back from death's door.

It was the beginning.

2

"In Dirt There Is Life"

George Washington Carver loved dirt. "People murder a child when they say, 'Keep out of the dirt!'" Carver says in *George Washington Carver* by Lawrence Elliott. "In dirt there is life."

In dirt, George Washington Carver found his own life, as well. Dirt and dreams were about all Carver had as a boy, and, as it turned out, they were about all he needed.

Carver's love for all plants — from the lowliest, thorniest weed to the most delicate, sweet-smelling rose — blossomed into an extraordinary knowledge. In the dirt, Carver found rocks, which he made his pets. In the sounds of birdsongs and the whispers of the wind rustling through leaves and grass, Carver found music. Eventually, he would combine his knowledge and his dreams in a way that would benefit the world for all time. But first, he had to find teachers who could answer his endless questions.

"My very soul thirsted for an education," he wrote later. "I literally lived in the woods. I wanted to know every strange stone, insect, bird, or beast. No one could tell me."

Neither the older Carvers nor the neighbors, not even the teachers he would have later in life, could answer all his questions. Many of the answers would have to come from Carver himself. Without teachers or tools, he learned to use what was at hand.

Frontier families had no time to spend on flowers, much less rocks. So young George had to find clever places to keep his pets.

"Day after day, I spent in the woods alone in order to collect my floral beauties and put them in my little garden I had hidden in the brush not far from the house, as it was considered foolishness in that neighborhood to waste time on flowers," he wrote. "And many are the tears I have shed because I would break the roots or flower off of some of my pets while removing them from the ground."

Early on, Carver devised ways to keep his plants alive through the harsh winters. He dug a little cellar in the ground for his choicest beauties, and on warmer winter days, he would uncover the cellar and lift his plants out for a bit of sunshine.

Then there were the rocks.

"Rocks had an equal fascination for me, and many are the basketful that I have been compelled to remove from the outside chimney corner of that old log house, with the injunction to throw them down the hill," he later wrote.

But, like many children, he didn't always do *exactly* as he was told.

"I obeyed, but picked up the choicest ones and hid them in another place," he said.

Carver managed to keep some of those rocks for his entire life.

He was a puny child. For years, his growth was stunted by his bad health, and he looked much younger than his age. His vocal cords were damaged by his illnesses (possibly tuberculosis), and he always had a high-pitched voice that sounded like a young girl's. However, Carver's constant sore throats and coughing bouts gave him some advantages. For example, Carver's brother, Jim, was strong and robust and spent his childhood and youth working alongside Moses Carver in the fields and woods, doing the heavy labor on the farm.

Because he was sickly, George often stayed behind to help Susan in the house. Her work was heavy enough, she thought, and without George's mother, Mary, Susan needed company as well as assistance.

Many a boy or young man might have balked at "women's work," but George jumped right in to help. He wanted to learn to do everything Susan did.

He cleaned and scrubbed, of course. And he also learned to knit, using turkey feathers for knitting needles. He learned to darn socks so expertly that Moses was said to have preferred George's darning to Susan's. George also learned to work with leather and became skilled at shoemaking.

Susan's most important task was food preparation, however. Farm families typically had little money and bought only items like coffee and sugar at the general store in town. This meant that all the other food had to be gathered as it grew wild, or else raised in a garden.

As a young child, Carver helped to grow vegetables and to prepare foods to dry for the winter. Vegetables that grew as roots (potatoes and onions) could be stored in cellars, but most food had to be dried. He shelled beans and peas for hours and sliced apples and other fruit to dry outside in the sun.

He loved learning to gather all the area fruits and nuts and berries that grew wild: fruits like plums and blackberries in the early summer and pawpaws in the fall. Pawpaw trees liked to grow along creek banks. Pawpaws are long and greenish brown and taste like a cross between a banana and an avocado. Pawpaws could be eaten as fresh fruit, used in cakes, or turned into pawpaw jam. When the pawpaws ripened, it was important to gather the fruit immediately, or an animal like an opossum would devour the tasty treats first.

Young George learned to cook meals using the fireplace: biscuits and cornbread, simple cakes and stews. From Susan he learned that his mother, Mary, had had a wonderful memory, just as he did. Whenever Susan had taught Mary a new recipe, she remembered it from then on.

Slaves had seldom been taught to read. In fact, it was against the law to teach slaves to read and write. This was one way whites kept control of slaves. Many poorer whites could not read or write, either.

George desperately wanted to learn to

read. He did have one book. Susan had given him an old, blue-backed speller that she had brought in a trunk from Ohio. He all but memorized the speller, but he wanted more.

The Carvers kept mostly to themselves. Moses did not like churches, which annoyed many of his churchgoing neighbors.

Young George was about ten years old when he first learned of prayer, he later recounted. A neighborhood white boy came over on a Saturday, and while they played, the visitor told George he was going to Sunday school the next day.

"He said they sang songs and prayed," Carver later wrote. "I asked him what prayer was and what they said . . . I only remember that as soon as he left I climbed up into the loft, knelt down by a barrel of corn, and prayed as best I could. I do not remember what I said. I only recall that I felt so good that I prayed several times before I quit."

For the rest of his life, Carver relied on his religious faith, as he did on his music and his rocks and plants. Now he had another tool, one that gave him an explanation for the visions that he had long had. He believed they were messages from God, like the ones he would receive through plants.

Throughout his life, Carver liked to tell the story of the first vision he remembered. He was a young child and he really wanted a pocketknife. He could not afford one, however.

Then one night, Carver had a dream. In the dream, he saw one of Moses Carver's watermelon patches. In the field was a partly eaten watermelon with a knife sticking out. The next morning George went straight to the field and there, indeed, was the watermelon with a shiny knife stuck in the side. From then on, Carver believed in his visions.

By this time, Carver had gotten a reputation in the community. His gift for plants — for getting them to grow and bloom, to diagnosing the problem when one became sick — earned him a nickname: the Plant Doctor.

Farmers might ask Moses Carver to send George over to look at their sick fruit trees, or their wives might ask Susan if he could tell them what was wrong with their roses. On one such occasion, Carver made a discovery that would forever change his life.

William and Elizabeth Ann Baynham lived on the next farm. George knew the Baynham property well. Moses Carver had bought George's mother, Mary, from the Baynham family, and George had heard that the man said to be his father was buried in the slave portion of the Baynham cemetery.

One day, one of the Baynham women sent word over for George to come take a look at the roses. They were ailing. They needed a visit from the Plant Doctor.

The problem was easy, according to later accounts of the episode. The roses had been planted in a spot where they couldn't get enough sun. So young George transplanted the roses, then went into the house to tell Mrs. Baynham what he'd done.

The kitchen was deserted. He called out but no one came. From where he stood, he could see into the dining room. There were the most amazing flowers on the walls: pictures that someone had painted. He had to see more.

Carver stood rooted before the pictures, memorizing every stroke and thinking of how he could make his own versions.

The Plant Doctor had discovered a new field — he wanted to be an artist.

From then on, he had a new mission. He learned that artists used brushes. He had no brushes, but he did have turkey feathers. Artists used paints, so he squeezed the deep purple juice from berries of the pokeweed, a plentiful plant that grew wild in the area, and carefully painted flowers on rocks and wood and tin. When he had no pokeberry juice, he took sticks and drew on the ground. Carver's new activity would nourish his soul for the rest of his life.

Every day, Carver thought of new questions. The church in the area was used during the week as a school. There were few African-Americans in that area of the county, and for a time George and his brother apparently went to the school with the white children. They were learning the basics of reading and writing. Then some whites complained, and the former slave children could no longer attend. George's dream of an education was dashed.

But, when George was about eleven, he and his brother, Jim, were allowed to walk to Neosho, the primary little town in the area, eight miles away. They happened to walk past a building where lessons were being taught. George peeked in the window. He could hardly believe his eyes. All the children in this school were African-American. This was a school that *he* could attend. There *must* be a way. He had to go to that school.

3

Setting Out to Seek
His Fortune at Eleven

Young George could not get the school in Neosho out of his mind. He learned that it had a name: the Lincoln School for Colored Children.

The seat of the county government, Neosho had been fought over repeatedly during the Civil War, which had ended only about ten years earlier. At one time, Neosho was called the "Confederate capital of Missouri." After the war, the Freedmen's Bureau operated in town for a while, helping freed slaves. The Lincoln School had remained after the bureau left.

George pleaded with Moses and Susan Carver to let him go to the school.

"But where would you live?" they likely asked. "How will you eat?"

They might also have asked about books and supplies, and medicine if he got sick. After all, young George had no job and no money, and no family or friends to care for him in Neosho. And he *was* only eleven.

None of this bothered George.

He was sure he could get a job. He knew everything he needed to know. After all, he knew how to wash and to iron, how to cook and to clean. He knew how to care for plants and make them grow. He knew how to darn socks and to repair shoes, how to knit and crochet.

Finally, tired of hearing the child's begging, the Carvers agreed. Yes, he could go. They were sure he would be right back — maybe even that very night.

So Susan cooked a lunch: some fatty meat slipped in between bread. George packed the food and a clean shirt and some of his favorite rocks, and slung the parcel over his back, probably on a little stick. Still small for his age, he looked even younger as he started down the dusty road. He turned and waved. He was off to seek his fortune.

The walk to town took young George most of the day. By the time he arrived at the school, the children and the teacher had gone home. The run-down building was dark. The thin little boy in the faded homespun clothes felt very alone. Where could he go?

Then George spotted a barn. There were animals inside, munching on hay. He climbed up into the loft and managed to fall asleep.

When morning came, George hurried to leave the barn before the owner might come in to tend the animals and find him, as well.

He went over to the school, but no one was there yet. He had eaten his only food the day before, and Diamond Grove, even if he went there, was hours and hours of walking away. He was getting hungry. He remembered seeing some sunflowers near the barn where he spent the night, and he knew that sunflower seeds were tasty. He picked some seeds and perched himself on a pile of kindling to wait for the school doors to open. A small house, set among flowers, stood nearby. The door opened and an African-American woman came out. She caught sight of George.

This time George had had a stroke of really good fortune.

Mariah Watkins was a midwife, a woman who helped women when they had their babies. She also did laundry for people in Neosho. Her husband, Andrew, did odd jobs.

"What are you doing here?" Watkins asked.

George told her about being from Diamond Grove and coming to the Lincoln School to learn all kinds of things.

"That boy told me he came to Neosho to find out what made hail and snow, and whether a person could change the color of a flower by changing the seed," Watkins later recounted. "Imagine! I told him he'd never find all that out in Neosho, nor in Joplin, either, and maybe not even in Kansas City. But all the time I knew he'd find it out — somewhere."

In the meantime, Watkins informed George that it was Saturday. The school wouldn't even open again until Monday. His heart fell.

But Mariah Watkins invited the child, still calling himself "Carver's George," into the house for breakfast and to meet her husband, Andrew.

"And don't call yourself Carver's George anymore," she is said to have told him. "From now on you're George Carver." Later on, to keep other Carvers from receiving his mail by mistake, he added the "W" as a middle initial.

By the end of breakfast, the Watkins couple had made a bargain with George. He could stay with them and attend school. In return, he would help Mariah around the house and with her laundry business. He was set.

For about nine months, George Carver stayed with the Watkins family and attended school nearby. As it turned out, he may have learned more from his hosts than from the school. The teacher, Stephan Frost, had few answers for George's questions. He mostly taught reading and writing at a very basic level.

George wanted to achieve more, of course, and Mariah supplied him with his first Bible. Now he had a book that would take him a long time to finish. Carver kept this Bible with him for the rest of his life.

In addition to her midwife practice, Mariah also treated people in the community with herbal medicines. This was an area that had long interested Carver. He quickly delved into learning her skills. The Plant Doctor in turn taught Mariah what the plants had taught him.

One day, George had a wonderful surprise — his brother, Jim, arrived in town. He'd decided to go to the Lincoln School, too. Jim Carver worked as a plasterer to support himself. This was a craft that involved mixing a paste and applying it to walls and ceilings for a smooth finish.

Unlike his brother, Jim was not a serious student. After he learned to basically read and write, he dropped out of the school and eventually moved on to another town. George Carver did what he would do for years: He looked for another school that might have more answers to the questions that just kept piling up.

Then one day, Carver heard that a local family was leaving for Fort Scott, Kansas. At the time, many African-Americans were moving to Kansas from former slave states, hoping to find less prejudice and better jobs. Yes, Carver could ride along if he helped with the chores and brought some food. There must be a good school there, Carver believed. So he said good-bye to Mariah and Andrew Watkins, took his small store of clothing, his beloved rocks, and his special Bible, and set out for Kansas.

Kansas had indeed been a free state before the Civil War, but this did not necessarily mean that African-Americans were welcome there during the late 1870s. Many whites in Kansas had not wanted slavery, but they had not wanted African-Americans in the state, either.

After the seventy-five-mile wagon ride to Fort Scott, Carver alighted from the wagon and set out to find work. It was late in the day. He was totally alone. He reportedly nearly starved before he finally obtained a job as cook for a well-to-do family.

The training and practice he'd received with Susan Carver and Mariah Watkins served Carver well. Carver had inherited his mother's gift for recalling numbers and instructions. So when his employer rattled off recipes to him, Carver remembered them perfectly. And soon he was adding new spices or an herb or two to each dish.

In the meantime, he'd spotted a school. Carver lived in a little space under the back steps of the house where he worked, and he saved every nickel he could.

By sometime in the spring, Carver had enough money to pay for a shack for a few months, with a little left over for food. He had already bought his books, which were very expensive for him.

He managed to go to school until summer, then he began working at odd jobs to save money for school in the fall. He did laundry for the hotel and for stagecoach riders; he delivered horses for the blacksmith shop. In the fall, he began classes again. This did not last long.

Many whites did not like the idea of African-Americans getting an education. It was still very hard for whites to go to school, and illiteracy, or not being able to read or write, was very common among both whites and African-Americans in the United States, and especially so in areas where the Civil War had raged.

Most of Carver's classmates in Fort Scott were white; they were also older than he was. He was new in town and no one really knew him. It didn't take long for bullies to take notice of the thin youth who was always alone.

One day after Carver left school, two white bullies stopped him and began to taunt him.

Where did he get those books? Did he steal them?

They pushed and hit Carver. Then the ruffians grabbed his books and just walked away with them, as if nothing had happened. They did this in plain sight of numerous whites on the street. None of the passersby came to Carver's aid.

Without books, Carver could not do well in school. It would take him months to save up enough money for another set.

Shortly after this incident, on the night of March 26, 1879, he was awakened by a lynching in progress. Earlier in the day, a black man had been arrested for an attack on a white girl. Every African-American in town was struck with terror: They feared a lynching was at hand. Often, when lynch mobs got started, they didn't always stop with one victim. Sometimes they looked around for others, as well.

Carver did not wait to see how the whites behaved afterward. He gathered up his small store of possessions and left town that night.

"As young as I was, the horror haunted me and does even now," Carver said decades later.

Unfortunately, this would also not be the only time he came close to a lynching.

4

The Prairie Years

In 1879, when George Washington Carver fled from Fort Scott, Kansas, he clearly wanted to put some distance between himself and the gory scene that he had witnessed.

Carver moved more than seventy-five miles away, to Olathe, Kansas, a town about twenty miles from Kansas City. For the next eleven years, he lurched from one prairie town to the next, sometimes in great despair and disappointment, sometimes with shimmering hopes of special schooling or a job that involved more than scrubbing other people's dirty clothes. But, regardless of what befell him, he would pick himself up, look for another laundry job, and move on.

In Olathe, Carver was lucky once more in finding a fine African-American family with whom he could live. Laundry was the key again, as he began helping Lucy Seymour with her laundry business. He moved in with Lucy and her husband, Ben.

Carver picked up new skills from Lucy Seymour, just as he had from Mariah Watkins. Lucy specialized in fancy ironing: shirts and blouses, petticoats and dresses with hard-to-iron ruffles and tucks and pleats. For a time, Carver just washed the clothes and watched Lucy from a distance. But as always, he observed every motion, and soon his fingers flew through every step in the new operation.

Ben Seymour was Presbyterian and very religious. George went to church with Ben, and they discussed the passages Carver read from the precious Bible he had managed to keep with him in his travels. Eventually, Carver joined the Presbyterian Church.

When the Seymours moved to Minneapolis, then another Kansas town, Carver followed. By this time, Carver had turned his skills into a business. He borrowed money from a local bank and set up a laundry operation in a ravine known as Poverty Gulch.

Along the way, Carver had managed to acquire an accordion and a harmonica and to learn to play them. He still painted and "fooled around with weeds." And, most important of all, there was a school he could attend in Minneapolis.

As usual, Carver was much older than the students in his classes. But he now had the confidence of a young man who had a successful business in town, who belonged to a local church, and who played his instruments for various community events.

Carver made friends this time. His schoolmates visited him at "George Carver's Laundry," the one-room shack with a little lean-to kitchen, that was both business and home-sweet-home.

After school, Carver's friends followed him home and "oohed and aahed over George's paintings and his collection of rocks and pressed wildflowers," Lawrence Elliott wrote in *George Washington Carver: The Man Who Overcame.*

Then one day during the last winter Carver was in Minneapolis, a printed letter from Mariah Watkins arrived. The news was not good. Jim Carver had died of smallpox in Seneca, Missouri, the summer before. She had just found out.

Carver was crushed. His brother was dead. When he rallied, it was with new determination.

"Being conscious as never before that I was left alone, I trusted God and pushed ahead," he wrote years later in *A Brief Sketch of My Life*.

Now he had a new dream: He was going to go to college. His questions would all be answered there.

Carver learned of a Presbyterian college in Highland, Kansas, so he applied for the fall term. After an agonizing wait, a special letter arrived. He was admitted! They would expect him to begin the fall semester in September of 1885. Carver was overjoyed. He knew he'd have to work his way through school, but he could *always* scrub clothes. Life was going to be marvelous.

Carver thought long and hard about how to make sure college was a success. He'd heard of a new skill called typing. He would learn to type.

In fact, a student who had once gone to high school in Minneapolis had opened a business school in Kansas City. So, once again, Carver set out. He spent his savings on a typewriter and painstakingly taught himself to type. He also learned shorthand. By the end of the summer, he was working the night shift at Western Union, typing in the telegraph office.

But before reporting to Highland, Carver decided to go to visit his brother Jim's grave and to see those he loved in Missouri. After all, life could be short, even for someone his age. He'd expected to grow old with Jim.

So Carver took a train south. He went to Seneca, where Jim Carver had died, and visited his brother's grave. Moses Carver had paid to have a tombstone erected for Jim. From there Carver walked the thirteen or so miles to Neosho and paid a call on the Watkins family. Then he trekked the eight miles to Diamond Grove, where he found the older Carvers much aged.

Moses Carver still worked some in the fields, but Susan Carver stayed in more than ever. They were delighted to see the tall, thin young man. A local doctor had told the Carvers that the sickly slave child would never live to be twenty-one. Yet, here was George, tall and relatively healthy and going to college, while his robust brother already lay in the cemetery.

When George left, the Carvers gave him the spinning wheel that his mother had used. He kept it with him for the rest of his life.

Then George Carver walked away once again, down the road he'd left as an eleven-year-old, when he'd faced an unknown future with only a few rocks and a clean shirt. But this time, George knew where he was going: He was going to college.

When he reached Highland, Carver asked to see the president. As he waited, he marveled at the brick buildings and the dark wood and the books. He had made sure he looked his best.

But, as things turned out, none of that mattered.

Not all his hard work and not all the courses he'd mastered.

Not his references.

Not his knowledge of shorthand and typing, skills that most of the students lacked.

Not even the fact that Carver was Presbyterian mattered.

The only thing that mattered was the color of Carver's skin. Highland did not admit Negroes.

"I was admitted, went, but when the president saw I was colored, he would not see me," Carver wrote in 1922.

Carver stumbled away. He was totally in shock. He had no place to go, not even for the night. He had no job and hardly any money. He knew no one in town.

He began walking.

Eventually, he came to a fruit farm owned by a family named Beeler. Yes, they could use some help with the laundry.

It took Carver a year to save enough money to move on from Highland. It would be nearly five years before he would again try to attend college.

One of the Beeler sons, Frank, moved to a largely unsettled area of Kansas popularly called "The Great American Desert," where he opened a store. Frank Beeler encouraged George Carver to move to the prairie. There he could homestead some land — a process where settlers obtained land from the government, lived there for five years, and then received ownership.

So Carver moved to the area of western Kansas that today is called Beeler. He went to work for another pioneer named George H. Steeley. Carver registered a claim for 160 acres in 1886, historians say, and began building a sod house in his spare time. Luckily, he continued to live on the Steeley property and was there during the winter. Blizzards are common in western Kansas, and many new settlers did not survive them.

* * *

Carver completed his sod house on April 18, 1887, according to one of his biographers, Linda O. McMurry. He moved in with only a cookstove, bed, cupboard, chairs, and laundry equipment.

In typical Carver fashion, he quickly mastered the techniques of sod construction and began adding improvements. Snakes and insects liked to live in sod houses. Some builders lined the walls in fabric, which rustled when critters slithered under it. Carver whitewashed his walls instead. He managed to grow splendid plants in the dry prairie soil.

He built a greenhouse and preserved his favorite plants through the winters. Visitors arriving in the deep snow marveled at the sight of bright, blooming plants inside the Carver house. Soon he was called for advice when a newcomer arrived and began a house.

Carver's neighbors on the prairie were overwhelmingly white, but these people accepted him. He was the most educated man in the area. He joined a church and a literary society and again played his musical instruments for socials. And, of course, Carver drew and painted. During his time on the plains, he saw a marvelous new plant and made a drawing on a scrap of paper. It was called yucca.

In Beeler, Carver also had art lessons, apparently for the first time. He took lessons from Clara Duncan, an African-American woman. She had taught at Talladega College in Alabama and later became a missionary for the African Baptist Episcopal Church, according to Linda O. McMurry, who conducted extensive research for her biography of Carver.

Carver traveled about doing various odd jobs that took him over a wide territory. Some reports say he traveled as far as New Mexico and possibly nearly to Denver. Wherever he went, he drew and picked up rocks and conducted numerous experiments with plants, ones that would serve him well in his later life as a soil scientist. And, he questioned. He always questioned.

Carver's abilities were recognized in Beeler, but he still seemed to have little chance of using his talents there. In March of 1888, a local newspaper, the Ness County *News*, wrote of Carver's gifts with plants and in art and geology. The article included a reference to his "collection of about five hundred plants in a neat conservatory adjoining the residence of his employer."

But a comment of the writer's must have made Carver's heart sink: "Were it not for his dusky skin — no fault of his — he might occupy a different sphere to which his ability would otherwise entitle him."

While Carver had achieved much in Beeler, he still hungered for a place that would allow him to develop his plants and his painting — regardless of his skin color. And he still had all those questions that no one had answered. So, in the summer of 1888, he borrowed three hundred dollars through George A. Borthwick, a local banker, using his farm as a guarantee he would repay the loan. Leaving Beeler behind, Carver set out again in search of more education.

Decades later, the Beeler townspeople would learn of Carver's accomplishments and erect a monument to him as "Citizen-Scientist-Benefactor . . . Ness County is proud to honor him and claim him as a pioneer."

Carver did laundry and odd jobs as he moved toward Missouri, apparently his intended destination. However, he had told everyone back home in Diamond Grove and Neosho that he was going to college. He could not bear to tell them that he had been turned down. So, as he neared the Missouri border, he instead turned north toward Iowa. Not far from Des Moines, he paused in a village called Winterset, where the hotel needed a cook. While Winterset looked much like many of the other towns through which Carver had passed, this place would be special to Carver. Here, at long last, he would encounter people who would not only recognize his talents, but would be instrumental in helping him reach his number one goal: to go to college.

George Washington Carver received a Masters of Agriculture degree from Iowa State College in 1896. In October of that year he became the Director of Agriculture at Tuskegee Institute, where this photo was taken.

When Carver began his career at Tuskegee, he expected to find a suitable laboratory awaiting him. That was not the case. Instead, he had to build one from scratch, using found objects from the local garbage dump to create the laboratory seen here.

Photo: Bettmann/Corbis

Carver with Henry Ford after being presented with a modern, fully equipped laboratory for food research, a gift from Mr. Ford. Here, Carver is showing Ford the products created from his plants, such as peanut butter.

Carver with President Franklin D. Roosevelt. Carver received the Roosevelt Medal for Outstanding Service to Southern Agriculture.

Carver often used strings and scraps of burlap to be knitted into useful items. He would make natural dyes for these objects from mulberries and walnuts he found on his nature walks.

Photo: David E. Scherman/TimePix

Tuskegee Institute president F. D. Patterson (left) watching as Democratic politician James Farley (right) talks with Carver.

Photo: Hulton/Archive by Getty Images

Carver working in his laboratory at Tuskegee. Much of Carver's lab equipment, displays, and experiments are on view at the George Washington Carver Museum located at the Tuskegee Institute.

Carver is shown here painting orchids on canvas. Painting was his first love, and he won numerous awards for his artwork.

5

Winterset and Simpson College

George Washington Carver said he strived "to do all common things uncommonly well." He displayed his determination to follow his own advice every time he dipped another dirty garment into soapsuds, ironed a shirt stiff with starch, or scrubbed yet another floor. At the same time, he pursued uncommon things in the frontier communities where he often lived.

He painted, though he had only the crudest materials and often made them himself. He sang, having a high-pitched, somewhat startling voice, as a result of all his respiratory illnesses. He taught himself to play musical instruments, beginning with cornhusk fiddles he made in the fields of Diamond Grove. He tinkered with plants, seeking their secrets and prodding them to perform in new ways for him.

While others saw Carver as pursuing an ever-changing array of new activities, Carver thought of himself as pursuing but one vision: a search for truth. In Winterset, Iowa, this vision began to come together. It would soon flower in a little town called Indianola, about twenty miles away.

Yes, Carver cooked again for a hotel and, indeed, the guests were pleased. Yes, he started a laundry again, and once again had more customers than he could serve. He went to church, of course, and sang.

But one evening in Winterset, someone truly heard him.

The choir director was a forceful woman in the community named Helen Milholland.

"The next day, a handsome man called for me at the hotel, and said his wife wanted to see me," Carver later wrote. "When I reached the splendid residence . . . I was most astonished when she told me that my fine voice had attracted her."

The Milholland home was filled with things George loved: pictures, books, and a magnificent piano. Even more amazing, a painting of a flower sat on an easel in the study, along with a palette of paint.

Helen Milholland painted, but her flowers did not appear lifelike. When Milholland complained that her painting did not look lifelike, Carver impulsively picked up a paintbrush, and, with a few strokes, solved the problem.

"You've painted them too far away," he is said to have told her. She and Carver struck a bargain: She would give him music lessons, and he would give her art lessons.

Soon the Milholland household was like a second home to Carver. He coached Helen Milholland with her art. He practiced voice and piano. He transformed the flower garden and read stories to the children.

Eventually, he told the Milhollands the painful story of his efforts to attend Highland College. They were appalled, but insisted he should try again — at Simpson College in nearby Indianola. Simpson would admit Carver. The Milhollands were sure of it.

Matthew Simpson, a Methodist bishop, as well as a friend of Abraham Lincoln, had provided funds to set up the college. Simpson was a firm believer in the equality of all men. When he applied this time, Carver informed the college of his color. He did not want a re-play of his experience at Highland.

Simpson College would indeed admit Carver, his letter of admission said. Not only that, but he would not be the first African-American to attend, though he would be the only one enrolling at that time.

So, in September of 1890, Carver set out for Simpson College. He would likely be the oldest student. Nobody there would be poorer. And he would doubtless be the only student also operating a laundry. Could he make it?

The answer was not immediate in coming.

Carver had saved every penny he could. But after he paid the school fees, he had only a few cents left.

"After all my matriculation fees had been paid I had ten c(ents) worth of cornmeal, and the other five c(ents) I spent for beef suet (hard fat)," he wrote in a 1922 account of this period. "I lived on these two things one whole week — it took that long for the people to learn that I wanted clothes to wash."

Carver had no money for student housing, but he managed to locate an empty shack where he could live. Then he arranged to buy on credit the simple equipment he needed for his laundry: tubs, a washboard for scrubbing the clothes, iron, soap, and starch.

Carver had asked the college president if the area could use another laundry. The school official assured Carver there was indeed a need for his business. Moreover, he told the young man that he would announce word of the new laundry in assembly. Then Carver waited . . . and waited. A week passed without customers. By this time, he had eaten all his food.

Luckily, he had written to the Milhollands about his plight. Helen Milholland contacted a friend of hers in Indianola, Mrs. W. A. Liston, who operated a bookstore with her husband. Mrs. Liston visited Carver's laundry and then called on the forgetful college president. He promptly made announcements and helped to send clients over to Carver.

When students found their way to Carver's shack, they often stayed to talk. They could not help but notice that he had no furniture. They sat on boxes he'd gathered from local stores. He did have a battered cookstove that he'd found at the town dump, where someone had discarded it as useless.

Carver never forgot what happened next. One day while he was outside of the shanty, some of his schoolmates visited. They'd taken up a collection and bought him a bed and a table and chairs.

Not only did Carver make friends at Simpson, he was hugely popular. He joined the literary society and was known for his humor and his penmanship.

Carver took the necessary academic subjects at Simpson, but his heart was in music and art. The art studio was a sight to behold. Easels and paintings were everywhere. The smell of oils and turpentine was almost overwhelming. Unfortunately, the idea of a male African-American art student was almost overwhelming to the art teacher, a young white woman who only recently graduated from college. Her name was Etta Budd.

Males typically did not study art at Simpson. African-Americans did not usually study it at all, since making a living at art was then very difficult. Moreover, there was an additional fee for art, which Carver had not anticipated. He could paint and he could pay the fees, he assured Etta. He just needed a little extra time to wash some more clothes.

Carver's determination prevailed. Soon he was not only painting, but he'd convinced his teacher that painting was in him.

Etta noticed something else about Carver — he had no coat. The Iowa winters were cold with heavy snowfalls. So she obtained an overcoat for him.

The bookstore owners, the Listons, looked after Carver as well, and he, in turn, took care of their flowers. They basically accepted him as a member of the family. Mrs. Liston referred to herself as "your mother" in her correspondence with him for the rest of her life.

He still experimented with plants, and one day he took Etta Budd a blue geranium. She was astonished.

He'd told her about many of his plant projects. She knew he was known for rising at four A.M. and going out to collect plants. His drawings of plants were beautifully exact. But a blue geranium? This was extraordinary.

Etta knew a bit about plants herself. Her father was J. L. Budd, a professor of botany, the biological study of plants, at Iowa State University in Ames, and she had taken botany herself.

Etta gathered together some of Carver's work and sent it off to her dad. After a time, she called Carver in to see her.

What did he plan to do after he finished school?

Carver answered that he would paint, of course, and he wanted to have a school for "his people."

But how would he earn his living?

Etta Budd had a plan. Her father had written, suggesting that Carver enroll at Iowa State University in the fall. He could pursue a degree in botany and have a career in agriculture. He could both make a living and make a contribution to others.

Carver was stunned — and devastated. How could he give up art? That was his love above all else. Yet his ideal had long been "to be of the greatest good to the greatest number of my people."

He just had not found a way to do it. Was this it? If so, would it really require him to give up the thing he loved the most?

6

Iowa State
University

Fortune smiled on George Washington
Carver when he enrolled at the State
Agricultural College of Iowa in 1891. At the
time, this was probably the most important
agricultural school in the nation. Even more
important, several of Carver's major professors and close friends would assume the most
significant national positions in agriculture
in the United States for decades to come.

Things did not look so promising in
Carver's first days at the new school, however. By this time, he was twenty-seven years
old, nearly ten years older than many students were. Once again, he was the only
African-American on campus. While the faculty and administration welcomed Carver, as
did most of the students, some people were

still racist. Occasionally, other students would call him insulting names.

Even worse were the problems he faced in housing and dining. The housing department could seemingly not find a space for him. Then James Wilson, one of Carver's professors and the new head of the Agricultural Experiment Station, the university operation that tested soils and plants, heard about the situation. Wilson promptly cleared his desk and moved his office upstairs, giving his space to the new student. Thus, Carver acquired a room.

Dining presented another challenge. Dining hall assignments were used to build social relationships among students, who received rotating assignments to tables in the dining hall. However, the dining hall manager sent Carver to eat with the help in the basement.

Word of Carver's treatment soon traveled back to his art teacher at Simpson College, Etta Budd. She is said to have contacted one of Carver's other friends, Mrs. W. A. Liston, who grabbed her hat and coat and took the train from Indianola over to Ames. She still regarded herself as Carver's "second mother," and she reacted like a mother hen whose chick has been threatened.

On arrival at Iowa State, Liston insisted

on seeing Carver's classes and his room. She met his professors, and that evening she stayed for dinner, following him down the steps from the handsome dining room to the area below. When the dining manager protested her eating with the staff and asked what the faculty and officials would think, she reportedly told him tartly that he should have thought of that before he assigned Carver's dining facilities. Moreover, she informed the manager that she expected to return again soon.

The manager didn't wait for Mrs. Liston's next visit to address matters. The next morning, when Carver started down to the basement for breakfast, he was asked to kindly join the other students. A place had been made for him at an upstairs table.

Soon Carver was a great favorite with students. He invented a table game that spread quickly through the hall and became a tradition at Iowa State.

If a student requested an item, such as salt, the response would be giggles and averted gazes — but no salt. Eventually, someone would ask for another item in Latin, and immediately the item would be passed over. By then, the student needing the salt understood the key to the code: to come up with the term in Latin.

Now and then, Carter still encountered prejudice, but it became rarer and rarer. He was popular at Iowa State, as he had been at Simpson. Money was an ongoing problem, but he was apparently not compelled to set up a laundry in Ames. Sometimes he worked as a janitor or a waiter on campus. He cleaned the greenhouse and the laboratories. And he made and sold hominy.

Hominy was yet another survival tool he carried from working in the house with Susan Carver. It was a fluffy white food made from dried corn, water, and a little lye, a strong liquid left after fireplace ashes were soaked in water. Hominy had helped sustain many settlers through hard winters. The pioneers had learned to make hominy from the Indians. It was messy to prepare, but it was cheap. So when Carver had no other means of support, he made and sold hominy.

He made nearly perfect grades in botany and horticulture, and achieved an excellent overall average. He did this along with working and sometimes having to take a break to go out and look for wild plants because he had once again run out of money for food.

Other students could not help but admire Carver's determination and hard work. He cut up wrapping paper to use for notes. Other students began saving their pencil stubs for him. But no matter the difficulty, Carver always pressed on.

Still devoutly religious, Carver started prayer meetings with other students. They began meeting with one of his professors, James Wilson. During 1893 and 1894, Carver traveled to Lake Geneva, New York, representing Iowa State at national Young Men's Christian Association (YMCA) meetings. Here he met and established long-lasting contact with students who would become leaders in church activities throughout the country. He was said to always take his specimen case along, looking for new plant samples in yet another environment.

Carver managed to participate in a wide range of what we could call extracurricular activities. He debated and joined a literary society, and acted in the school plays (sometimes taking women's roles because of his voice). His vocal high notes may have been a problem in his speech, but they were a great asset in singing. He was a welcome addition to the college quartet and even was offered a scholarship to the Boston Conservatory of Music.

Somehow he also assumed the job of official trainer for the school athletic teams and appeared to have a special gift for massage.

Required to join the National Guard student battalion, Carver first suffered the comments of its commander, General James Rush Lincoln, for his slouch, the result of bending over laundry tubs all his life. But even his bones had to bend to Carver's determination.

He added a two-mile walk to his day, holding his hands together behind his back, marching with a stick lodged between his armpits. Within two years, he'd achieved captain, the top student rank. General Lincoln took note.

"This most gentlemanly and efficient cadet has risen to the rank of captain through personal determination and merit alone and I couldn't be prouder of him," he said.

Despite all his accomplishments, there were still those who tried to make him feel inferior. Sometimes he still met with heckling and name-calling, particularly when he participated in events in public, such as when he served as a military escort to the governor of Iowa.

Carver knew how to live with prejudice and hardship. Something else tore at his heart. When he decided to give up painting as his life's work and "help my people," he was so brokenhearted that he put away his brushes. No longer did he envision himself as going to Europe to study art one day. So he did not paint for some time after leaving Simpson College.

However, he soon began painting signs for social events and then set up his easel and began to paint again. Taking a vacation was not something George Carver did. So when winter break came, he returned to Indianola and took more painting instruction from his former art teacher, Etta Budd.

During the winter of 1891–1892, Carver created some of his best work. His specialty was flowers, of course, and the roses and peonies bloomed for Carver while the midwestern winter raged outside.

He recalled his sketch of the yucca plant that had so fascinated him during his trips around the plains. Now it grew tall again and blossomed under his skillful brush strokes. *This* truly was a vacation.

Carver intended to return for more lessons at Christmas in 1892. However, over-work and scrimping on food caught up with him in the fall. He became very ill, reportedly suffering from anemia, a serious condition that occurs when the body does not produce enough iron in the blood.

Before Christmas, Carver's professors asked him about entering some of his paint-ings in a statewide art exhibit being held in Cedar Rapids shortly after the holidays. He could not possibly afford the trip, he said.

Then one of his professors asked Carver if he'd like to earn a little money cleaning his house after Christmas.

As he started to leave for the house, how-ever, a sleigh full of Carver's fellow students pulled up and offered him a ride. They seemed in great spirits and, to Carver's dis-tress, turned away from campus and headed into town. They paid no heed to his pleas to drop him off first.

When the driver did stop, they were in front of an expensive men's clothing store. Carver did not want to go inside in his worn-out work garments, but the boys paid no mind. Not only did they hustle him inside, they found a beautiful gray suit and insisted he try it on.

The more he protested, the more items Carver's friends located for him: gloves and a hat, socks and a shirt and tie. Carver already had a new pair of shoes. Professor Wilson had been so upset about Carver's thin, ragged shoes one cold, wet day that he had peeled some bills from his wallet and ordered Carver to go buy some new shoes. Last of all, the friends added a black overcoat and whisked Carver out the door.

By this time, Carver was really dismayed. The group reportedly sang Christmas songs to drown out his frantic questions about how he would pay for all of these items. They ignored his calls to take him to his job and instead pulled up to Professor Wilson's house.

Finally, Carver thought he could get someone to listen to him. Inside with Professor Wilson was Professor J. L. Budd, Etta Budd's father. The two men didn't seem at all surprised by Carver's visit. But they told him they couldn't require the students to drop him off to clean his professor's house. Instead, he was to go directly to Cedar Rapids. They not only had a ticket ready for him, but

Professor Budd had gone to Carver's quarters and picked up the paintings his daughter had suggested he enter.

But how could he repay the money?

He couldn't, they told him. His teachers and classmates had each contributed to send him. They wanted George Carver to represent them all.

And he had to go, they said. His work was already listed in the catalogue: G. W. Carver, No. 25: Roses; No. 43: Peonies; No. 99: Yucca gloriosa; No. 186: Vase of Flowers.

Carver turned away in tears. But no time for that — he had to catch a train.

All four of Carver's paintings won awards, but the one of the yucca was one of the winners to represent Iowa at the Chicago World's Fair in 1893. In Chicago, Carver's yucca won honorable mention for Iowa.

Carver's goal of a college diploma was fast approaching. By this time, Carver's professors realized what the farmers of little Diamond Grove had known long before: George Carver had extraordinary gifts with plants. He was especially skilled in determining the best soils and fertilizer for each type of seedling. Moreover, he was already becoming an expert in grafting, or attaching part of one plant onto another so the parts would grow together.

Graduation from Iowa State came in 1894 for Carver, who received a Bachelor of Agriculture degree. He was approximately thirty years old. Carver's "second mother," Mrs. W. A. Liston, came to graduation, accounts say, bringing with her a bouquet of red carnations from his friends at Simpson. And, according to researcher and writer Lawrence Elliott, "(Carver) put one of the blooms in his lapel and, to the best of anyone's knowledge, wore a flower, a sprig of evergreen, even a weed — some small growing thing — every day of his life."

The Iowa State faculty had no intention of losing Carver, however. He had become much too valuable. He presented and published papers on grafting and flower bulbs in state publications. He even found the time to improve the campus flower beds. It was no wonder that one professor called Carver "the ablest student we have here."

So the faculty in Carver's department asked him to join them as an assistant in botany and to take over the greenhouses. In addition, he could study for his master's degree. There would be no need for odd jobs or laundries or peddling hominy. This indeed must have seemed like heaven to Carver. And Ames, Iowa, was likely the closest place to heaven that Carver would come on this earth.

7

A Vision to Serve
My People

George Washington Carver flourished in graduate school at Iowa State. His skills in plant breeding brought him respect from faculty members. Assigned to work with a nationally known expert in fungi (plants like mushrooms and molds, which lack the pigment that colors most plants green), Carver discovered he had a special talent in this area. Iowa's Agricultural Experiment Station began printing Carver's articles in their bulletins. He was a popular teacher of freshman biology classes.

As time for graduation neared (he earned a master's in agriculture in 1896), Carver began to receive job offers. Alcorn Agricultural and Mechanical College (known as Alcorn A & M), a Mississippi school for African-Americans, offered Carver a faculty position.

Iowa State wished to keep him on their staff. Professors wrote glowingly of Carver's work and his contributions to the college. Carver's lifetime habit of early morning plant gathering paid off at Ames. He donated more than 1,500 of his finds to the university plant collections.

One of Carver's professors, L. H. Pammel, was a famous authority on fungi. Pammel called Carver "the best collector I ever had in the department or have ever known."

Staying at Iowa State, where he was not only successful and beloved, was highly tempting. But what of Carver's vision? He believed his destiny was to do something to help others of his race. After all, he'd given up the pursuit of a career in painting and an opportunity in music to follow a higher calling. He hesitated, unsure of which course to follow.

Then a man named Booker T. Washington entered Carver's life. Washington was a well-known African-American who'd gone from Virginia to rural Alabama, where he had started a school for blacks. It was called the Tuskegee Normal and Industrial Institute, which meant that it trained teachers and prepared students to become skilled in trades in use at the time, especially in construction. Students learned to build wagons and make bricks, to build houses and barns, to weave baskets and to fashion brooms.

By this time, Carver was achieving a reputation in agriculture. He was already considered the most learned African-American in agriculture in the United States. Washington wanted Carver to come to Tuskegee to establish and head a school of agriculture. This would be a great service to African-Americans, Washington said. These were the most persuasive words Washington could have used.

Carver had long believed he had a destiny to contribute to his race. Back in the days when he first left Diamond Grove and lived with Mariah Watkins in Neosho, Missouri, she had told him he had an obligation to his fellow African-Americans. She had also told him about the slave Libby who had taught her to read, even though she might have been severely punished, even killed, for her action. At that moment, Carver was said to have had one of his visions, an image of helping others in a similar way.

So to Carver, Washington's offer appeared like a destiny, one that he had to fulfill. In April of 1896, Carver wrote back to Washington.

"(I)t has always been the ideal of my life to be of the greatest good to the greatest number of 'my people' possible and to this end I have been preparing myself for these many years; feeling as I do that this line of education is the key to unlock the golden door of freedom to our people."

Iowa State's staff tried to keep Carver, but many of his friends and colleagues were unsure how wise that was. They knew of Carver's mission to help his race, and they did not want to stand in his way.

Thus, it was with a sorrowful heart that many on the Iowa State staff watched Carver leave for Alabama. They pooled their money and bought Carver a microscope to take to Alabama. It would be virtually his only piece of equipment there, and he would use it for the rest of his career. Carver himself, with his cheerful attitude and willingness to make do with what he had, had no idea what sacrifices he was making in order to go to Tuskegee. He would soon find out.

*   *   *

Tuskegee was located in what is called the Black Belt in Alabama, named for the rich black dirt in the area. This soil had attracted plantation owners to the area before the Civil War, and they, in turn, had brought in large numbers of slaves to till the soil. Now much of the land suffered from too much planting of the same crop, cotton. Many people, white and black, could barely exist on what they earned.

Carver knew he was going into an area he knew little about, a former slave state where the rules for African-Americans were many and seemed to apply to all aspects of life. While he had sometimes experienced insults and prejudice in Missouri and Iowa because of his skin color, most residents accepted him as an equal citizen, and community institutions were almost always open to him. The opposite would be true in Alabama.

Slavery had ended about thirty years before Carver arrived in Alabama, but schools, including colleges, were still segregated in the state and would be for well over another half century. Schools for blacks were pitifully funded and maintained. Blacks could not eat in restaurants where whites ate, try on clothes in stores whites used, or attend churches with whites. While blacks often cleaned and cooked for whites, they did not eat with them or visit them, unless it was to stand at the back door.

Tuskegee Institute had been built with great sacrifice, against great odds. Several wealthy whites had contributed money to help start the school, but Washington and the teachers he hired had done much of the work themselves, along with the students.

Washington offered Carver one thousand dollars a year, plus his room and board, which included all his expenses except travel. This angered many of the teachers already at Tuskegee, where salaries were less than four hundred dollars a year. There was also a great educational gap between Carver and the other teachers at Tuskegee. According to some accounts, Carver was the only staff member to hold an advanced degree from a white college in 1896. Carver was indeed giving up a great deal to go to Tuskegee, and he expected to be treated like the accomplished academic that he was.

The Tuskegee faculty had other ideas. In their eyes, Carver had no "practical" experience. He no longer appeared to be the "washerwoman" that some had termed him for much of his life. They did not see the man who had worked for a blacksmith and built sod houses and cooked and washed his way across much of America and through a long line of poor schools.

Instead, the other professors saw a cultured, gentle man who set out his easel and brushes to paint, who got up at dawn to go out and pick little weeds, and who expected to have larger quarters assigned to him than they had. He said he needed them for his "collections."

There was another difference between Carver and the other faculty members and most of the students: Their skin color was much lighter than his. During and after the plantation system, blacks who had some white ancestry tended to receive better opportunities. In turn, some lighter-skinned African-Americans considered themselves superior to darker African-Americans. So in Tuskegee, Carver faced not only prejudice from whites but from blacks, as well.

When he arrived and went to Washington's office, however, Carver had high hopes. He looked out the window, as he later described it, and saw a landscape of red and yellow gullies — big ruts in the land, where water had washed the soil away.

At that moment, he had another of his visions. He saw not the bare, ugly gashes in the land, but rolling green fields, where food grew in abundance. He would teach the African-American farmers of the area to farm the land in new ways and to use all the good things that nature provided free. The land would renew itself, the farmers would become prosperous, and their children and grandchildren would reap opportunities their elders never had.

Many aspects of Carver's vision would come to pass, but he would not necessarily receive the credit that he thought he deserved, nor the good will and support of his fellow faculty members.

While Carver was known for ignoring the latest styles in clothing and for wearing his garments until they literally fell apart, he always wore a flower in his jacket lapel. When he arrived in Tuskegee, as the story goes, his lapel held a pink rose. This was definitely not the dress of the usual arrival.

Soon after he came, Carver wrote to Booker T. Washington, the president of the school, asking for additional space for his belongings. He already had a room to himself, while other single faculty members were expected to share a room. He also revealed that he expected to stay at Tuskegee for only a limited time.

"I came here solely for the benefit of my people, no other motive in view," he wrote. "Moreover, I do not expect to teach many years, but will quit as soon as I can trust my work to others, and engage in my brushwork, which will be of great honor to our people showing to what we may attain, along science, history, literature, and art."

He apparently planned to stay at Tuskegee for about five years doing his good deeds. Then he planned to go to Chicago to study art. These dreams were not appreciated in Tuskegee, where survival was uppermost in the minds of most people. In fact, rather than bringing Carver honor, such comments tended to put distance between him and his fellow teachers.

Carver had little time to worry about diplomacy, however, as he immediately discovered there was virtually no equipment at the school for his new laboratory. He had not only been hired to establish a program that did not exist, he was given no tools with which to build it. One thing was certain, however: Booker T. Washington had indeed chosen probably the only person in America who could accomplish the task.

Drawing on his lifelong skills at using what he had — usually dirt and junk — Carver set to work. He fashioned beakers from drink bottles. Later, after automobiles became more plentiful, he taught his students to make crucibles, containers used to melt substances, from hubcaps. They were also learning one of Carver's most important lessons: There is no waste in nature.

8

Looking for Ways to Help the Poorest

At Tuskegee, George Washington Carver set about looking for ways to help the poorest of the poor. Though thirty years had passed since the end of the Civil War, the majority of southerners, black and white, were still very poor. The war created much damage in the South, and rebuilding was very difficult.

In many places, practically all the public buildings, such as schools and churches, had been destroyed. Coaxing enough food out of the soil to feed their families was a full-time job for most people. They did not always succeed. Many people starved or fell sick and died from lack of good food and medicine.

Iowa and the other states in the North had suffered little damage during the war because the battles were mostly fought in the

South. When he arrived at Tuskegee, Carver had to completely rethink what he could do there. First and foremost was to help people to feed themselves. Here Carver called upon his lifetime habit of using the riches of nature to make up for a lack of money. This technique served both Carver and his students well.

The professor still rose at four A.M. to pray before setting out to look for plant samples. Now he also scouted the countryside carefully to discover the wild fruits and nuts, berries and plants that people might gather for free. Plum trees grew in abundance, for instance. Children and birds nibbled at the small, juicy fruits when they were in season, but, otherwise, little use was made of them.

Oak trees were common to the area, as well, and in the fall they dropped their acorns inches deep on the ground. Indians had used acorns wisely, pounding them into a kind of flour. Carver began issuing bulletins from the experiment station. The first one was on feeding acorns to hogs. Others examined ways to use plums, cowpeas (black-eyed peas are one variety), and sweet potatoes for human food.

Carver's first group of students only numbered thirteen, but the class grew nearly six times that by the second semester. Carver was on his way.

Booker T. Washington, the head of the school, had begun holding conferences for farmers soon after the school was started in 1881. These events had begun to draw large numbers of farmers, black and white, by the time Carver arrived. As head of the agricultural school and the experiment station, he had an opportunity to demonstrate his ideas to the people who needed them most.

Just as enrolling at Iowa State had been a stroke of luck for Carver, he was blessed again with having had several professors there who would become secretaries of agriculture for three U.S. presidents. These three men would set farm policy for decades. The first of these contacts was the professor who had given up his office to Carver, James Wilson. Wilson became Secretary of Agriculture under President William McKinley.

Carver had stayed in touch with Wilson, as he did with the majority of his former professors. Wilson believed in Carver and in his work, but he was often frustrated in his efforts to help him. Segregation of the races was the reality in much of the country, either by law in the South or by practice in much of the North. With so few resources available in the South, the whites in charge there saw that the benefit of most public money went to whites. There was usually little or no trickle-down in public services to blacks. This was true in assistance to farmers, as well.

Carver's relationship with Wilson was invaluable in getting at least small amounts of support to Tuskegee. Congress dispensed federal money for state agricultural schools, but white southern Congressmen used a variety of methods to see that practically all the money went to white colleges that did not even admit black students. Some of them did not admit women, white or black. Even though James Wilson was Secretary of Agriculture, he could not overcome the directives of the U.S. Congress.

However, Wilson could do a few things on his own. For instance, he learned that he could dispense seeds. The USDA (United States Department of Agriculture) typically dispensed free seeds through the offices of members of Congress, who gave them out to voters in their areas. This was one tool the politicians used to get themselves reelected. Blacks were prevented from voting by a variety of means, so southern Congressmen saw no need to hand out free seeds to African-Americans.

Wilson sent seeds to Tuskegee, however. By the early 1900s, twenty-five hundred or more packages of seeds, each containing ten packets, were finding their way into the hands of area farmers, sources say.

Carver also began offering short, practical courses to farmers, usually for two weeks at a time. He taught farmers how to fertilize their crops using natural fertilizers and how to test seeds. He demonstrated how to get the best results from different types of soil and encouraged farmers to bring in samples from their own farmland. After a time, farm wives came along with their husbands. This presented another opportunity.

Carver realized that while farmers grew food, they did not necessarily know how to prepare it well. He began developing recipes for commonly available foods, such as sweet potatoes, peanuts, and cowpeas, as well as for wild greens. He experimented with ways to pickle and preserve foods, including meats, because spoilage was a big problem. Such methods were necessary because electricity did not become available in much of the South until 1939. (The George Washington

Carver Museum at Tuskegee has a large display made up of the foods Carver pickled and canned to show to farm families.)

While Tuskegee's president, Booker T. Washington, had long sponsored well-attended farmers' conferences each year, Carver began holding monthly meetings for farmers. They could come and go home in one day. These meetings became very successful.

Still, Carver was only reaching a small fraction of the farmers he wished to contact. He decided to load up a farm wagon and to take his classes to the farmers. Often he would go to churches and meet with members after services.

Some European countries had begun to use "movable schools" to reach farmers, so Booker T. Washington suggested Carver might develop this method for Tuskegee. Carver jumped at the idea and began expanding it. Washington obtained funds for the project from Morris K. Jesup, a banker in New York, and others.

By 1906, the Jesup Wagon, as they named the vehicle they created, was calling on general stores, fairs, and churches, loaded with equipment, information, and displays. Thousands of farmers took advantage of the demonstrations.

The project caught the attention of Seaman Knapp, a special agent with the U.S. Department of Agriculture. He eventually was able to get the Smith-Lever Act passed through Congress in 1914. This set up funds for demonstration agents. Eventually, nearly one thousand black agents were hired, along with thousands of white ones.

The more contact Carver had with poor farmers, most of whom had no land of their own, but simply worked on the land of others, the more he tried to find a crop that would replace cotton.

Cotton had been the major cash crop since before the Civil War. It drained the ground of nutrients, the minerals the soil needed to renew each season. But people needed a crop to sell for cash. Carver was already encouraging farmers to plant legumes — plants with pods, like peas or beans — to restore worn-out soil. And he encouraged farmers to grow peanuts. Cotton crops were becoming infested with an insect called the boll weevil. (Bolls were the large seedpods that held the cotton.) Boll weevils didn't attack peanuts. So gradually, Carver concentrated his research on two crops — the peanut and the sweet potato.

Carver developed hundreds of products

from peanuts, including drinks such as peanut lemon or orange punch; face creams and lotions, shaving cream and soap, and even a dandruff cure; dyes and stains for wood, leather, and cloth; medicines; and numerous foods for people and animals.

Amazingly, Carver developed milk from peanuts, a product desperately needed by children allergic to cow's milk. Letters of thanks from mothers around the world expressed their gratitude.

Today many children eat Carver's most popular product: peanut butter.

Among Carver's tastiest recipes are ones for peanut butter candy, peanut brittle, and peanut chocolate fudge (included at the back of this book).

From sweet potatoes, Carver concocted everything from after-dinner mints to instant coffee, chocolate, and orange drops; from mock coconut to vinegar and yeast; from alcohol and medicines to paints. He developed writing ink from the sweet potato itself and then made paper from the vines.

Turning again and again to dirt, Carver created numerous dyes and paints, including ones from Alabama clays. One variety of blue was said to be a color thought lost, last reproduced in Egyptian tombs. Using such products, Carver also managed to sometimes teach art classes at Tuskegee.

Carver did not limit himself to research on sweet potatoes and peanuts, however. He studied alfalfa and soybeans and promoted them to southern farmers, who long after his death would make the two plants major crops in the South. Carver also made concrete from cotton, and rubber from goldenrod, the "weed" that grows wild and has bright yellow fall flowers.

All of Carver's research was done in a "laboratory," where it was good that he did not need to follow strict scientific procedure. After all, he had hardly any "scientific" tools with which to work.

Yet this lone individual working with students in an out-of-the-way place in Alabama was not only becoming known to Americans and people around the world, he was gaining the attention of some of the world's most famous inventors. Several pleaded with Carver to join their laboratories. They offered the Alabama professor the use of some of the best equipped research facilities in the world and a high salary, as well.

Thomas Edison, the inventor of the lightbulb and the phonograph, reportedly offered Carver a six-figure salary if he would join him in his laboratory. Later on, Carver became friends with Henry Ford, who produced Ford automobiles. Ford tried very hard to tempt Carver to join his laboratory in Michigan. While Carver did develop products that Ford apparently used, such as synthetics from soybeans, Carver remained at Tuskegee. (In Carver's old age, Ford had an elevator installed to ease the elderly inventor's trips from his quarters to his lab.)

Mail from all over the United States and abroad poured in to Carver, who labored to reply, often with little help. In 1929, a supporter of Mahatma Gandhi arrived at Tuskegee in search of Carver and a special vegetarian diet for the great Indian leader, whose health was suffering. Carver created one, of course, and Gandhi went on to lead the nonviolent struggle that threw the British colonizers out of India.

Speaking invitations also flooded Carver's mail. He had long been a polished speaker. He had learned to delight audiences with humor and skits during his days of moving about the country and joining whatever literary society he could find. This usually went over well with the public, which tended to take Carver's remarks with the same good humor with which they were delivered. But every once in a while, someone took Carver's remarks too seriously.

The New York Times once wrote a sharply worded editorial about comments Carver made while speaking at a New York City church.

"I never have to grope for methods," Carver had told his audience. "The method is revealed at the moment I am inspired to create something new."

Then he added, "No books go into my laboratory."

The *New York Times* article, entitled "Men of Science Never Talk That Way," said that Carver's words revealed "a complete lack of the scientific spirit."

By this time, Carver had created hundreds of products from the peanut, using the only tools he had: laboratory supplies mostly made from junk, his intuition, and prayer. He was not about to be pushed off course by a few discouraging words. So Carver wrote the newspaper back on November 24, 1924, discussing the "gross misunderstanding" that had occurred over "divine inspiration."

"Inspiration is never at variance with information," he wrote. "In fact, the more information one has, the greater will be the inspiration."

In the last words of his letter, Carver stated one of the basic principles that guided all his work, from art to agriculture: "Science is simply the truth about anything."

9

Teaching Congress a Lesson

George Washington Carver was unique among the great inventors of his day: He gave his ideas out freely. People began to realize they could make money using Carver's products, and he was much in demand as a speaker.

Just because Carver was becoming well known did not mean that he did not still face racism, however. He might be invited to speak before an all-white group, for instance, yet be directed to take the elevator that carried freight instead of the passenger elevator.

Many whites still believed blacks and whites should not eat together, so Carver usually made arrangements to eat elsewhere, even if he were addressing a banquet.

Carver, like other African-Americans of

the time, could never be sure how whites would treat him. Sometimes whites, even in the South, invited him to stay with them and he did so. But Carver might stay in the home of southern whites during one week, and his life might be in danger the next. Sometimes he actually had to take care not to be attacked.

He had never forgotten the lynching he witnessed in Fort Scott, Kansas, before he attended college or the time he was in great danger in Ramer, Alabama.

The Ramer incident had occurred about ten years after Carver had arrived at Tuskegee. Carver was in his late thirties and had taken the train to the small Alabama town, where a photography exhibit was being held at a school for blacks. On board, Carver met a white photographer, a woman named Frances B. Johnston, who was also going to the exhibit. She was traveling around the South, photographing black schools.

When the train reached Ramer, a black male teacher met the photographer and escorted her to a local hotel. Blacks and whites did not mingle socially in the South, particularly with the opposite sex. So, when Johnston and the teacher reached the hotel, they encountered a crowd of whites, who began shooting at them. When the teacher fled, Johnston remembered Carver and managed to locate him. She helped Carver get to the next station to catch a train.

Gangs of whites roamed the area for days, looking for the black teacher who had to flee the town. Carver himself had to walk nearly all night to stay out of the mob's reach. Then he managed to board a train about six miles away.

Carver wrote Booker T. Washington that this was "the most frightful experience of my life . . . and for one day and night it was a very serious question indeed as to whether I would return to Tuskegee alive or not as the people were thoroughly bent on bloodshed."

By the 1920s, Carver had come to both national and international attention. In 1916, he was elected a Fellow of the Royal Society for the Encouragement of Arts in London.

Carver's continued efforts to promote the peanut had also begun to pay off. Many farmers had taken Carver's advice and switched from cotton to peanuts. They banded together in associations of growers. In 1921, the American peanut market was threatened by the availability of cheaper peanuts from outside the country. This meant that people who used peanuts to produce candy or snacks or other products could buy the nuts at a cheaper price from farmers outside the United States.

American growers asked Congress to pass a protective tariff, or tax, on the foreign peanuts, so American growers could keep their home market. Then they asked "Dr. Peanut," as Carver was sometimes called, to travel to Washington and speak to a committee of the U.S. House of Representatives.

Segregation of the races was still the reality in much of the United States. African-Americans were barred from attending many colleges and universities, especially in the South, so they seldom could get the education to entitle them to be an expert in any field.

Therefore, some members of the committee were impatient with Carver and did not expect him to be worth much of their time. The committee chairman, Joseph W. Fordney, a Republican from Michigan, told Carver he had ten minutes to speak. What happened next was remarkable.

Carver had amassed a sort of show-and-tell for the Congressmen. He took out breakfast foods, chocolate candy, salted peanuts, sweet potato syrup, and various combinations of products and displayed them before his audience. By this time, Carver was a master not only at speaking but at creating superb exhibits and displays, using all his considerable artistic talents. Once he had caught his audience's interest, Carver began to speak.

Calling the sweet potato and the peanut twin brothers that cannot and should not be separated, Carver called them "two of the greatest products God has ever given us."

"If all the other foodstuffs were destroyed . . . a perfectly balanced ration with all of the nutriment in it could be made with the sweet potato and the peanut," he said. "From the sweet potato we get starches and carbohydrates and from the peanut we get all the muscle-building properties (protein)."

By this time committee members had numerous questions, which Carver answered thoroughly and with good humor. Finally, the chairman said, "Go ahead, brother, your time is unlimited."

By that time, Carver was demonstrating milk and instant coffee from peanuts, and oils from both products. The peanut growers received their tariff on foreign peanuts, and Carver became nationally famous.

Yet, no matter how well known he became

or how much acclaim he received for his research, Carver collided again and again with the racist attitudes and practices of his fellow Americans. Unfortunately, these experiences did not only occur in Alabama or in the South; they might rear their ugly heads on the Plains or in the North.

In one famous incident in 1930, Carver was in the midst of a three-state speaking tour. Over several weeks, Carver spoke at meetings of scientific groups, YMCAs, black schools, and the Oklahoma State Teachers Association. He even addressed a joint session of the Texas legislature. Yet as always, eating, sleeping, and traveling proved difficult. So Carver arranged to get sleeping accommodations on a train traveling from Oklahoma City to Dallas.

There was no problem until Carver and his traveling secretary, H. O. Abbott, arrived. Once rail officials saw their skin color, they refused them service in the sleeping cars. Instead, they had to ride all night in a coach car, which was segregated and had no sleeping compartments. By this time, Carver was in his mid-sixties and was still facing the same racial battles he'd fought in his youth.

The president of the railroad apologized to Carver, but the policy continued.

Hotel stays could be frustrating. Carver's assistant always wired ahead and received acceptances for reservations. Yet there was no guarantee that the approval would be honored once they arrived and the color of their skin became evident.

In 1939, when Carver was in his midseventies, a well-known New York hotel received worldwide publicity for its treatment of Carver, who had traveled to New York for a national radio broadcast on a show called "Strange As It Seems."

Despite having copies of their reservations, Carver and his assistant were denied rooms. This time Carver refused to leave. He said he would wait. The hotel finally provided a chair near the men's restroom in an upstairs hallway.

Carver's assistant telephoned Doubleday, Doren and Company, which was publishing a biography of Carver. Company officials tried to get hotel officials to change their minds, but they would not budge. At that point, they called the city's newspapers, including *The New York Times*. At one point, a Doubleday vice president came to the hotel, promptly received a room, and tried to give it to Carver. However, the hotel staff blocked the exchange, declaring that they had no room available, after all. By this time, news reporters were writing stories about the elderly, world-famous scientist having to sit in the hall. The publicity was very bad for the hotel, which finally gave Carver his room, more than six hours after he had arrived.

As Carver entered his late seventies, his health declined considerably, and he seldom left Tuskegee, where the rich and the famous, the poor and the troubled, came to see him. People with a variety of illnesses came, looking for remedies. Poor farmers and rich businessmen came. Princes from England and Sweden came. President Franklin Delano Roosevelt dropped by, stopping to see Carver during a tour of the South. Vice President Henry A. Wallace came to visit Carver more than once.

Carver's friendship with Vice President Wallace lasted half a century. As a child, Wallace, who was renowned for his own plant breeding, had watched Carver graft plants at Iowa State. There Carver had taken him thither and yon, over hills and through brambles, looking for mushrooms and plant diseases — a young man and a small boy who would together have a remarkable impact on agriculture.

Wallace always referred to Carver as the "kindliest, most patient teacher I ever knew," one who "could cause a little boy to see the things which he saw in a grass flower."

10

Enlarging the Human Spirit

George Washington Carver's greatest gift may have been his ability to reshape his vision of himself and his place in the world in the face of crushing loss. As a child, when he was turned out of the church school in his own neighborhood because of his color, he threw himself into his private garden; his plant "beauties" had no concern for his skin.

When he finally made it into an art program and his beloved teacher told him that a black man had no future as an artist, he resolved to help members of his race to better themselves through agriculture. He went to Tuskegee to teach students and develop crops to reform the pitifully poor lot of southern farmers, rather than staying at Iowa State in his beloved greenhouses, where he was already making a name for himself in plant science.

Yet, all his experiments and efforts at Tuskegee appeared to help the peanut industry and manufacturers more than tenant farmers (those who farmed other people's land). Moreover, Carver had long believed that if he showed what an African-American could do in agriculture and art and music, then whites would recognize the foolishness of their prejudice. But after his appearance before Congress, Carver was world-famous — and he still often faced the same racist practices he had seen as a child in Missouri.

African-Americans still could not attend many universities, even the public ones supported by the taxes of all Americans. Even Carver had trouble staying in hotels, getting sleeping quarters on trains, being served in restaurants and sometimes even at luncheons and dinners where he was the speaker. So, for one last time, Carver shifted his vision again.

He began to focus more and more on what would decades later become known as organic farming, and he began to work more directly in efforts to improve race relations. Finally, he became convinced that he had to leave a record of his work so that others could benefit from it. So he gave his entire life savings, more than sixty thousand dollars, to set up the George Washington Carver Foundation, which established the museum at Tuskegee.

Everyone around Carver knew stories about how little money the plant professor spent. He kept his checks in his desk drawers for years sometimes, yet he often gave money to students and others who needed it. He wore the same clothing for decades. In fact, when Tuskegee unveiled a bronze bust of Carver on campus in 1937, he reportedly was wearing the same dark gray suit he had received from the faculty and students at Iowa State nearly forty-five years earlier.

Carver was always very clear about what mattered in life and in science. So when the museum set about to mount Carver's work, he insisted they include everything: his rocks, his paintings, his embroideries and his wood carvings, his food displays and exhibits, his experiments and his inventions.

Carver's death had been expected for years. He had begun to physically weaken in the 1930s and had been expected to die a number of times. Yet each time he rallied, getting out of bed to go back to work. And he did not pass away until the museum was ready.

Tuskegee had donated an old building that had once been the campus laundry. The building had been redecorated and became a National Park Service monument to a man who had spent so many years as a laundry-man.

There was another irony in Carver's museum, as well. Carver had loved his art above all else, particularly his paintings of flowers. But several years after his death, a museum fire destroyed most, but not all, of Carver's paintings.

Indeed, in dirt there was life, and Carver's work with plants remained intact. That could not be destroyed. The art and magic of George Washington Carver were preserved as one whole: Sometimes the plants were painted with pokeberry juice on tin, but often his work continues today in products such as peanut butter or peanut oil. His ideas have not only lasted, they are just beginning to be appreciated.

Reforestation, growing fruits and vegeta-bles using natural fertilizers, and using nat-ural insect predators to kill harmful pests (such as ladybugs to eat aphids) are all ideas

Carver continued to advance, even as he grew more and more feeble.

One January morning in 1943, when Carver was nearly eighty, he neglected to take the elevator Henry Ford had installed for him. He fell down a flight of steps and was found later by the woman who had come to prepare his breakfast. When he died a couple of days later, on January 5, 1943, people came from far and wide for days to honor the man who had gone so far because of his questions and his determination.

President Franklin Delano Roosevelt sent a message, as did his vice president, Henry A. Wallace.

In death, as in life, Carver was surrounded by flowers. And as usual, he wore a flower in his lapel. A white woman in Tuskegee had pleaded with Tuskegee officials to provide the blossom — a white camellia — from a bush that Carver had cured years before.

Tributes to Carver poured in. Senator Harry S. Truman, the U.S. senator from Missouri who later became president, and U.S. Representative William Short sponsored the legislation to create the George Washington Carver National Monument at Carver's birthplace, Diamond Grove, Missouri. Today, the

National Park Service operates the extensive national park dedicated to Carver in Missouri, as well as the George Washington Carver Museum at Tuskegee University.

Generations of Americans, black and white, have encountered the teachings and the products developed by George Washington Carver. Stamps and coins carry Carver's likeness. Buildings and submarines display his name. In 1977, he was enshrined in the Hall of Fame for Great Americans.

Probably even more to his liking, his ideas on organic farming, on recycling, and on using natural fertilizers began to be put into practice nationally and internationally during the 1980s. Fittingly, NASA selected Tuskegee as one of two sites to develop foods for use in outer space.

George Washington Carver would likely not be surprised at the increasing use of his ideas. After all, it was Carver who would always send visitors on their way with a flower or a few seeds.

When the George Washington Carver National Monument, located on the original Moses Carver farm in Missouri, was dedicated, the New York *Herald Tribune* wrote:

"Dr. Carver . . . triumphed over every obstacle. Perhaps there is no one in this century whose example has done more to promote a better understanding between the races. Such greatness partakes of the eternal. Dr. Carver did more than find hidden merits in the peanut and sweet potato. He helped to enlarge the American spirit."

George Washington Carver's Recipes*

Peanut Butter Candy

2 cups sugar
2 tablespoons peanut butter
½ cup milk

Blend all ingredients together, boil for 5 minutes, remove from the fire, and beat steadily until cool. Break into pieces and store covered.

Peanut Brittle

3 cups granulated sugar
1 scant cup boiling water

*From the George Washington Carver Museum at Tuskegee University

¼ teaspoon baking soda
1 cup roasted peanuts

Melt sugar, boiling water, and baking soda in a pot over a slow fire. Cook gently without stirring until a little hardens when dropped in cold water; add the nuts; turn the mixture into well-buttered pans and cut while hot. Stirring will cause the syrup to turn to sugar.

Peanut Chocolate Fudge

1 cup cream
2 cups white granulated sugar
¼ cake unsweetened chocolate
1 tablespoon butter
1 cup chopped peanuts

Put the cream and sugar in a pot over a slow fire, and when this becomes hot, put in the chocolate, broken up into fine pieces; stir vigorously and constantly; put in the butter when it begins to boil; stir until it creams when beaten; remove and beat until quite cool, and pour into buttered tins; add the nuts before stirring.

Sources

George Washington Carver monument near Beeler, Kansas. http:// skyways.lib.ks.us/ counties/ns/gwcarver.html

George Washington Carver Museum, Tuskegee University, Tuskegee, Alabama. http:// www. cr.nps . gov / csd / exhibits / Tuskegee / gwcmuseum.html

George Washington Carver National Monument, National Park Service, Diamond, Missouri. http://www.nps.gov/gwca/index.html

George Washington Carver Papers, original in Booker T. Washington Papers, Library of Congress.

Elliott, Lawrence. *George Washington Carver: The Man Who Overcame*. Englewood Cliffs, N.J.: Prentice-Hall, Inc., 1966

James, Larry A., and Linda Petty James, comp. *Diamond: The Gem City. A History of Diamond, Missouri, and Marion Township.* Newton County, Mo., Historical Society: Litho Printers, 1995.

Kremer, Gary R. *George Washington Carver in His Own Words*. Columbia, Mo.: University of Missouri Press, 1987.

McMurry, Linda O. *George Washington Carver*. New York and Oxford: Oxford University Press, 1981.

Massey, Ellen Gray, (ed.). *Bittersweet Country*. Garden City, N.Y.: Doubleday, 1978.

Means, Florence Crannell. *Carver's George*. Boston: Houghton Mifflin Co., 1952.

About the Author

CAMILLA J. WILSON teaches journalism at Minnesota State University Moorhead. She has written for newspapers and magazines for more than twenty-five years. She has spent considerable time in Asia, where she has written about social and political issues from China to Bangladesh. She spent more than two years in Vietnam during the war there and wrote for a group of small newspapers. She has written *Rosa Parks: From the Back of the Bus to the Front of a Movement*, also published by Scholastic Inc.